It Happened to

Bullied

Interviews by
Angela Neustatter and Anastasia Gonis

Photography by
Laurence Cendrowicz

W
FRANKLIN WATTS
LONDON•SYDNEY

First Published in Great Britain by
Franklin Watts
96 Leonard Street
London
EC2A 4XD

Franklin Watts Australia
45-51 Huntley Street
Alexandria
NSW 2015

ISBN: 0 7496 5387 6

A CIP record for this book is available from the British Library.

Printed in Malaysia

Series editor: Sarah Peutrill
Art director: Jonathan Hair
Design: Steve Prosser
Photographs: Laurence Cendrowicz (unless otherwise stated)
Picture credits: Photofusion: 16, 30 Tina Stallard; 26 Ute Klaphake; 35 Joanne O'Brien; 42 Sam Scott-Hunter.
Matt Hammill: 18, 21, 23, 24.

With grateful thanks to our interviewees and Emily Lovegrove.

Contents

Introduction

What is bullying?

Bullying can mean a lot of different things - from being called names, being teased about your appearance, being threatened or physically abused, or having your possessions stolen and thrown around. It can come from people you see as friends, schoolmates, or even adults.

What are the effects?

Bullying can make you feel scared or upset. It might affect your school work, your self-esteem or your relationships with other people such as your parents.

Why do people bully?

There are many reasons why people bully. They may do it to feel powerful or look 'cool', but often it is because they are jealous or even scared themselves.

Does bullying matter?

Statistics show that children who are bullied are more likely to leave school early. They may also remember, and be affected by, the bullying for many years.

Bullies themselves are also affected by their behaviour in later life. They are more likely to get court convictions, and have antisocial personalites than people who did not bully as children.

What can be done about it?

Everyone - children, teachers and parents - needs to recognise that bullying, in any form, is unacceptable. Schools should have anti-bullying programmes that allow children to report bullying without being concerned about any consequences.

Real life

This book features the real-life stories of five young people who have experienced bullying and one young woman who was bullied and later became a bully herself. Because bullying can be so distressing, some of the interviews include the thoughts of one of the child's parents.

The interviews are written as closely as possible from the words of the interviewee. They are written in Question and Answer format (Q and A). Alongside them you'll see some interesting facts and figures and talking points, which should help you to start thinking about some of the more complex issues. The names of some of the interviewees have been changed.

If you are being bullied:

◆ Write down what happens to you. Make a note of the dates, places and times you were bullied and exactly what happened. This will make it easier to tell people about it.
◆ Think up some good replies to the comments people usually make to you.
◆ At breaktimes try to stay where an adult can see you.
◆ Tell someone what's happening – perhaps a teacher, or your parents, or phone one of the helplines listed on page 46.

If you are a bully:

◆ Try to think about what effect your behaviour has on the person(s) you are bullying. How would you feel in their position? Reading the interviews in this book is a good place to start.
◆ Think about why you are a bully. How does it make you feel? Do you really enjoy it?

If you have seen bullying:

◆ If your friends bully others try to talk to them about their behaviour.
◆ Don't just join in with bullying.
◆ Don't just ignore it because you are worried you might yourself be bullied.
◆ Tell an adult and encourage the bullied person to speak up as well.

It Happened to Simone

Simone, 15, lives with her mother and baby brother. She was badly bullied by a girl at her comprehensive school, and others turned against her. Simone and her mother, Michelle, describe what happened.

Q When you were moving from primary to secondary school, were any friends going with you?

A One girl, Janie, wanted to come to the same school as me and I felt good about that, even though my mum didn't particularly think of her as a good friend of mine. She always thought Janie was a manipulator and not very nice, but I didn't feel worried by that.

Q Were things happy at first at secondary school?

A For the first year it was fine and Janie and I got on well. Then when I was 14 things changed. Janie wanted me to go out with her one day but I was already going out with someone else. The next thing, she was shouting at me because I'd gone out with this other girl and not her. She left a very nasty message on my phone.

Q How did that make you feel?

A I was a bit stunned. I kept my mobile switched off the rest of the day.

> "Very few people wanted to be friends with me."

I made the effort to be friends with Janie because she didn't have a lot of other friends. But then she managed to persuade Lizzie, a friend of mine for a long time, to turn against me.

Q That must have been very hurtful. Was it just Lizzie who turned against you?

A No. She and Janie then told lots of the other girls - the boys at school didn't get involved in this - that I wasn't a true friend, that I did lots of horrible things. And it worked. Very few people wanted to be friends with me. It made me very miserable.

Q Did you do anything about it?

A After a few weeks I told my class tutor. She called a meeting with me and Janie but Janie just sat there swearing and saying I was a liar and had made it all up. She stormed out of the meeting.

A (Mum): The staff didn't do anything to penalise Janie for that. I phoned afterwards and asked the tutor what she was planning to do. They told me they were going to leave it and see if the trouble fizzled out. She said she had told Janie to keep away from Simone. I wanted the mothers of Janie and Lizzie - she was very much with Janie, although she wasn't quite as bad - informed. The school said they didn't want to do that.

Q Did things improve after this, Simone?

A No, they didn't. Janie said lots of horrible things about me. I had a few friends, and they were loyal, thank goodness. In playtime we kept out of Janie's way, but she did things like calling me on my mobile and saying she would tell people I set on Lizzie, which I never did.

Q Did you go to your tutor again?

A I went to my class tutor four times but she didn't really take it seriously.

It's a Fact that...

Only 25% of students report that teachers intervene in bullying situations, while 71% of teachers believe they always intervene.

90% of adolescents who were bullied believed that the victimisation caused them significant problems, including feelings of isolation and hopelessness.

Bullying has been found to be used as a strategy to establish dominance in new peer groups as the students enter a new or bigger school.

"... she would phone my mobile and say she was going to beat my mum up."

Her attitude was it's just girls being bitchy and it'll pass if left alone. But it didn't.

Q So the nastiness went on?

A Yes. Later in that term I had a haircut and when I went into school Janie told the other girls to come up to me and say I looked like a nun. I said, 'But nuns don't have any hair,' and Janie said, 'Exactly.'

A (Mum) I didn't know exactly what was happening but I was aware of the effect it had on Simone. Her behaviour was changing. She was a lot more angry than usual at home. If I asked her to do chores or anything, which she had always done very willingly, she would shout. If I asked what was wrong she'd say nothing. Her mood had an effect on her brother and her nan.

Q Was the bullying just at school?

A No. Out of school Janie would come to where my nan lives because I often go and spend time with her. She would hang around outside, and she would phone my mobile and say she was going to beat my mum up. Another time, when I was picking up my little brother from school, Janie and Lizzie and some other girls followed me. They waited outside my brother's school and, when I came out, they said in loud voices, 'Oh look, there's Simone.' I took my brother's hand and said, 'Let's walk fast.' Every time I looked round Janie would be looking at me and she'd say 'Yes? What? What?' She was bringing up her hands as though she was going to fight with me. They followed us all the way to my nan's. My brother was frightened and I felt intimidated.

A (Mum) I was very upset when Simone told me about this. I informed the head of year and Simone's tutor the next day, but their response was that it had happened out of school and they couldn't do anything. I asked them to involve the parents. They didn't want to do that because they thought the mothers would hold it against each other. I got the impression they were actually scared of having trouble with the parents. And still they were saying, 'It's just girls' stuff,' and 'They'll get over it.' But I could see how unhappy Simone was.

It's a Fact that...

Bullies tend to come from homes where there is poor supervision, and tolerance of aggressive behaviour.

Bullying plays a huge part in the reasons pupils' give for leaving school.

> "I felt very unsupported at school and I was also afraid if I made too much fuss I'd be accused of telling tales"

Q How did your friends react?

A It made them very angry that Janie and Lizzie and the others were being so horrible and they told me to go to the teachers. But by this time I didn't see the point. I felt very unsupported at school and I was also afraid if I made too much fuss I'd be accused of telling tales and no-one would talk to me.

Q How did this affect your feelings about school?

A I didn't want to go to school. Some mornings I'd tell Mum I didn't feel well and she'd let me take a day off. But I didn't want to change schools either. I'd always liked lessons there and done well. Besides, I felt that would mean Janie and her lot had won. I didn't see why I should be forced out.

Q So things just went on like this?

A Not exactly. One day a friend and I went outside at lunch time and a group of girls were there led by Janie who shouted 'Who are you looking at?' They were swearing at me and going on and on. My friend said, 'Take no notice.' But then Janie shouted. 'Just walk away like you always do!' and something snapped. I shouted back at her and we got into a big argument. Then a teacher appeared and separated us. I walked around the corner and burst into tears.

A (Mum) At that point I felt it was enough. The school had to take seriously what was happening. I wrote a letter to a school governor and she got in touch with me and then the headteacher called me in. He thought that, because Simone hadn't made too much of an issue of it, she was allowing the girls to do this to her. That it was attention-seeking. I was furious. I said I didn't agree. Then he asked me if she was being physically bullied and I said no, and he told me he didn't really call what I had described bullying. He too took the view it was girls being girls and would fizzle out.

It's a Fact that...

Many students tease their peers to go along with the crowd but feel uncomfortable about their behaviour.

Q Simone, did you know your mother was going to the head?

A No, I didn't know. In fact I didn't tell my mum many of the things that happened at school because I knew it would upset her. But afterwards the head of year must have told Janie something because she said to everyone, 'Simone's been grassing again.' Then the whole school seemed to know Mum had been to see the head.

A (Mum) Perhaps it wasn't right to go to the head but I was really worried. I'd seen Simone becoming more and more withdrawn. She seemed to feel very alone and her school work was slipping. I said to the head, 'Are you telling me these girls have to inflict physical damage on Simone for you to take it seriously?' I believe mental scars are serious. You hear of children just putting up with bullying and then they end up committing suicide.

"... [the headteacher] didn't really call what I had described bullying."

Q Did the head have any suggestions?

A (Mum) He did suggest putting Simone into a different tutor group, but I pointed out this wouldn't really help because a lot was happening outside the classroom. The thing I was adamant about was wanting the mothers involved. His view was the girls would then be worse, but I know the mother of Lizzie and she has high expectations. I'm certain she wouldn't be happy about her daughter being caught up with Janie, who comes from a very different kind of home. And I think parents should know how their children are behaving at school.

Q How long has the bullying gone on?

A It's been about six months but it has calmed down a bit now. The trouble is it's calmed down before then started up again. I only really feel all right at school when Janie and her friends aren't there. The other day when they were away a friend said, 'Simone, that's the first time I've seen you really smile in a long time.' Sometimes I do

"... I think parents should know how their children are behaving at school."

feel very angry and want to lash out at them but I know I'd get suspended if I did.

A (Mum) I feel I've taken the first step by writing to the governor and I've got to go on fighting for Simone's happiness. I can see that taking her out might be an answer, but it would be a shame because she loves her lessons and always did really well until this started. So for now I've told her to come and talk to me, and not bother with the teachers when things are difficult, and I'll do what I see best. I don't want to move her but if she becomes more unhappy, I'll have no choice. As a mother I have to decide what is best for her happiness. ■

The names of Simone's bullies have been changed.

Talking Points

- Simone does not feel the school was supportive enough. Do you agree with the school that Janie and Lizzie were just 'girls being girls', not bullies at all? Are verbal comments less serious than physical assault?

- Do you think telling a bully's parents about their behaviour is helpful? What should they do?

It Happened to Benjy

Benjy, 11, lives in London, UK with his parents and sister and has suffered racial bullying at school. He was also bullied because he was small and had learning difficulties. He describes the experience and his parents, Herman and Agnes, explain how they tried to support him.

Q Were you bullied from the time you started at primary school?

A I went there when I was five and, although when I first went there some kids pushed me around a bit because I was small, it wasn't bad. I made friends and felt happy.

Q When did things go wrong?

A I had difficulties with lessons. I couldn't keep up with the other children. The teachers said I shouldn't worry. But in the second year my parents got worried because they could see I was struggling all the time trying to keep up. My dad said it was strange because my verbal abilities were so good. Children were starting to call me dumb.

Q So what happened then?

A My parents took me to a psychologist to do an assessment and he said I was dyslexic and had difficulties with numeracy.

A (Dad) it was clear to Benjy's mother and I that he

was unhappy and beginning to feel different to other children. I presented the school with the psychologist's report but they didn't take a lot of notice. My impression was they regarded dyslexia as something the middle-classes use as an explanation when their children aren't doing as well as they would like.

Q Did the bullying get worse?

A As well as calling me dumb some children teased me about being small. They did it when the teacher wasn't there and I didn't like to tell. Then one day they pushed my jacket down the toilet. I pulled it out but I felt very upset and alone and I wondered what I had done to deserve this.

"... I felt very upset and alone and I wondered what I had done to deserve this."

It's a Fact that...

It is often the child's reaction to that first encounter with being bullied which determines whether or not he or she will be approached again.

Direct bullying has been seen to increase through the early school years, peak in the middle school years and decline in high school years.

Q What was the worst of the bullying?

A There were very few black children in the school and the hardest thing was being bullied about my colour. And I was abused because my dad is German.

Q So what did children say about you being half-German?

A When the German football team was playing England they called me a Nazi - that sort of thing. And one time after there had been a documentary about Anne Frank, some children asked me why 'we' had been so cruel to her. When we did World War Two history children said things to me and I felt bad.

Q Were the things they said about you being black as bad?

A Just as bad and I felt that they would never forget I was black because I was different to all of them. Once in art when I drew a picture of myself one of the children said it looked like a monkey. Another one said I was dark because I'd been burned at birth. And I was really upset when a boy said my mum had been having a poo when I was born. That's the kind of thing they said. Just the other day when I was in the lunch queue a girl said to me, 'Black people have to go to the back.'

Q Did the bullying you describe happen regularly or just sometimes?

A It happened most weeks I was at the school. I wondered if I was going to be bullied when I went in and I felt very miserable because I thought I was the only one being laughed at.

Q Did you have friends to help you?

A I had a few friends but they couldn't really do anything.

"... I felt very miserable because I thought I was the only one being laughed at."

It's a Fact that...

Students who are physically different are more likely to be bullied than those who do not do well at school work.

Students often report that teachers seldom or never talk to their classes about bullying.

Q Did what was happening affect your behaviour?

A I was very frustrated and angry. I wasn't very good at controlling my temper. One time I got so angry I beat someone up for saying bad things. So I was getting into trouble at school and being told to see the headteacher.

Q Did your parents know what was happening to you?

A Yes, they did and they were sympathetic but I was going home with a bad attitude and having tantrums. Or I would take my anger out on my sister.

A (Mum) Of course we didn't like this behaviour but it was very clear Benjy was distressed a lot of the time. There were times when I felt really angry with the school because they didn't seem to make any effort to deal with what was happening. When the boy said Benjy's self-portrait looked like a monkey I was very shocked and we felt the teachers should speak to his parents, but they didn't. So then his father and I did and the parents were very sorry. They had no idea their son was doing this. They spoke to him.

Q What effect did that have?

A It was 100 per cent better afterwards. We became friends and the boy didn't bully me any more.

"It didn't seem to me that the teachers took any notice [of the bullying]."

Q So the school didn't do much to deal with the racist bullying?

A It didn't seem to me that the teachers took any notice.

Q Do your parents talk to you about racism?

A They talk about discrimination and the way some people speak about black people and some of the things that happen in the world. They tell me about the good things black people do and how special some people like Nelson Mandela are. We talk about it quite a lot at home.

A (Mum) I see Benjy facing the same issues I did as a child and I think nothing has really changed much.

Being left out by the other children can be just as painful as being physically abused.

(Benjy's mum continued)

I don't feel the school does enough to help minority children understand the value of being different and to help their peers value it too. The saddest thing is that Benjy was brought up with a strong sense of who he is as a mixed race person, but his confidence and sense of identity were rocked to the foundations at that school by what happened. Sometimes he was so low and I felt the pain for him when he asked over and over, 'Why do they do it?' But the school never let him know they understood that he was suffering racism, that it's wrong and that they would fight it. In my view the school didn't do enough to protect Benjy.

"In my view the school didn't do enough to protect Benjy."

It's a Fact that...

Children don't have to be a different colour to suffer racist bullying. Being from a different country can have the same effect.

Q Have your parents been able to do anything to help other children see positive things about being a minority race?

A Both my parents attend school activities, and Mum who comes from Nigeria is involved quite a lot.

A (Mum) I go in and talk to the children about black history from way back, the contribution they have made in the world up to the present. It's my way of trying to educate children to see that everyone has a place in society.

Q How much longer do you have at this school?

A I am leaving at the end of term and moving to secondary.

Q How do you feel about that?

A My parents have spent quite a lot of time looking at schools with me and we've chosen an all-boys school that has a good atmosphere. And it's got a strong racial mix and there are people from different ethnic backgrounds on the staff. I already go there for Saturday music and I know a few children.

Q So you are looking forward to it?

A I am. But I can't help feeling worried in case I'm bullied again. ■

Talking Points

◆ Benjy's story illustrates how, once bullies have chosen a victim, they pick on the most conspicuous differences and use these. But Benjy's mum thinks there's value in being different. Do you? Is it better to be 'normal' or an individual? Is it worth changing yourself, if you can, to fit in?

◆ Benjy couldn't understand why he was being bullied. Why do you think it happened to him? What do the bullies gain from it?

◆ Children can be very cruel bullies. Where do you think they learn this behaviour from? Adults, friends, the media – or is it a quality they are born with?

It Happened to Madeline*

Madeline*, 15, has been physically and verbally bullied by a schoolmate, and emotionally bullied by a teacher. She attends a private Catholic Girls College in the suburbs of Melbourne, Australia.
*not her real name

Q When did the bullying begin?

A It started after the first two weeks at school and it continued on a daily basis, till really late in the year. I was teased constantly for anything and everything, and was made fun of by another girl in my class. It was as if she had singled me out to make life difficult for me. I think it was because I was smarter than her, so she picked on me all the time. There was never a clear reason. This particular girl focused mainly on me. No other girl had serious problems with her. There was another girl whom she teased about her hair, but mostly it was directed at me.

Q Why do you think she acted like this towards you?

A I think it was because I had more friends than she had. Also she did it to call attention to herself. We were both new students to the school. We even looked alike. I mean, our features were so similar - even our skin tone was the same and all the teachers got us mixed up at the beginning.

When my mother came to the school, they thought it was the other girl's mother, and she had to keep repeating, 'I am Madeline's mother, not the other girl's mother,' over and over.

Q How did you feel towards your classmate after these attacks?

A Well, at the beginning, I tried not to care when it was just verbal bullying because all the class was on my side, supporting me. They knew who was at fault. But I was annoyed when the bullying became regular. My mother had to keep coming to the school to see the teacher. It interrupted her work-life and my classes.

"She was angry all the time and tried to relieve how she felt by picking on me."

It's a Fact that...

There is often more bullying in private schools than in state schools.

Students who regularly display bullying behaviour are generally defiant or oppositional towards adults, are anti-social and apt to break school rules.

Q Was anything done to stop this girl's behaviour?

A Nothing, except calling my mother to the school. The girl was reprimanded of course, but that didn't stop her. The teachers had discussions with us about how I could cope with it. They talked about the reasons *why* this was happening. This girl had a lot of behavioural problems. She was an attention-seeker. She was angry all the time and tried to relieve how she felt by picking on me.

Q Did you ever retaliate in the same way?

A I never physically touched her, but I always had a response for her when she verbally attacked me. I couldn't stand by and just take it.

Q How did your parents react?

A They had long discussions with me. They were patient and supportive. I would go home in tears and we would talk it through. They suggested I stay right away from her.

Q Could you stay away from her?

A No, she always found a way to get close to me. She was in my class, so it was difficult to avoid her. The teachers positioned her right away from me, but there was always some contact, whether it was going to the lockers, down the corridor or something similar. They promised me that we would be separated with the new school year and that's what happened. She was put in another class this year.

It's a Fact that...

People generally bully others when they are upset about something themselves, jealous of the other person, or trying to look 'cool'.

Q *Were there any other types of bullying by this girl?*

A Yes. There were two episodes of physical bullying. The first time she was making fun of the way I was swimming. She attacked me, kicking me quite violently, when we went to our lockers to change and get our lunch. My leg was badly bruised and quite sore for a long time. The second time, she elbowed me in the side, quite violently. My body was bruised over my lung area and my mother was afraid that I had internal bleeding. She took me to the doctor to be checked out.

"My body was quite bruised over my lung area and my mother was afraid that I had internal bleeding."

Q *What happened then?*

A Things didn't come to an end until I came home with the bruising over my lung. My parents informed the school that the police would be told because things had got out of control. They were ready to remove me from the school and to make a formal complaint to the Education Department. They felt, apart from the emotional trauma I was suffering, they were paying for a service, and not receiving what they were paying for. That was another issue. It was then that the school psychologist got involved and tried to sort us through our feelings.

Q *How did these events affect you?*

A I had low morale and low self-esteem. I didn't want to go to school. I thought the only solution would be to leave and go to another school. I didn't want that because I had made lots of friends and I was very popular. I also missed out on a lot of Maths classes because I had to go to see the counsellor during Maths class. I couldn't make up the lost time alone, so I had to get a private tutor to help me pass my subject.

Q *Was the reason why she bullied you ever resolved?*

A The school psychologist did assessments on both of us. I believe I now know the reason why. It's because her parents don't get along together. She comes to school very upset every day, and says that if she wears a simple ring or some other thing that her mother doesn't agree with, her mother hits and abuses her, and forces her out of the car. She says that she's not allowed to have the door to her room shut, that it must remain open at all times. She also has two younger siblings who get all the attention and she is totally ignored. So, after hearing all this stuff and seeing her scream during her violent outbursts, I realised that she must be abused at home. There is nowhere for her to get rid of her anger except at school. Unfortunately, I am the one that she has picked to pay for it.

Q Does your classmate have any friends at all?

A She doesn't have any at all this year although she had one last year. She just hangs out in the bathrooms during breaks and in all her other spare time.

Q This year, is anyone else being bullied by this girl?

A Only people with learning disorders. They're the ones being picked on this year.

Q Did you ever feel pity for her, seeing her act this way and knowing the reason behind it all?

A I didn't last year, but I do this year. I heard her threaten to kill herself. She actually said it to me. There was one instance when she was banging her head on the wall till blood was pouring down her face. She was sent to the school psychologist. That was when I felt pity for her.

"There was one instance when she was banging her head on the wall till blood was pouring down her face."

> "The teachers did their best to be patient with her but she was frequently sent out of the classroom."

Q What was her behaviour like in the classroom?

A The teachers did their best to be patient with her but she was frequently sent out of the classroom. One day, in English class while we were studying literature, (she has Attention Deficit Disorder) she went and hid in the cupboard. The teacher was calling out the class names and when her name was called, she jumped out of the cupboard. She has this habit of yelling, singing or talking while the teacher is conducting lessons. This particular day, she ate a huge box of Cheezles [a cheese-flavoured snack] for lunch, and when the teacher had had enough of her disruptive behaviour, she took the girl's hand and led her from the classroom. All the while the girl screamed, '*It's the Cheezles, I tell you!*'

Q Tell me what happened with the teacher?

A It was later that year. A male teacher kept on picking on me for absolutely no reason. Everything I did was wrong. I would do my assignment and he would order me to repeat it, saying it wasn't good enough, or not long enough. When I repeated the work, he'd tell me again that it still wasn't acceptable. I repeated one essay three times. When I questioned it, he reacted very negatively towards me, telling me I must do as I was told.

Q Did you tell your parents?

A Yes, they told me to do as he asked and that he would probably get tired of it, but he didn't. Even after the parent/teacher interviews, he continued the same way for quite some time. He even refused to call me by my correct name, which I hated being shortened, as nobody ever called me anything but my full name. But this teacher would call me everything but, and one day, prompted by my classmates who kept saying, 'Tell him to stop, tell him to stop,' I stood up in class and asked him to call me by my name. He simply

It's a Fact that...

Children who were named by their school at age eight as the bullies were often bullies throughout their lives. These children later had more court convictions, more alcoholism, more antisocial personality disorders and used more of the mental health services than the other children.

ridiculed me, and continued to be sarcastic and cruel towards me for some time. Finally, he did start using my correct name.

Q How long did this teacher act in this manner towards you?

A For a full term, and two weeks into the new term. I went to the co-ordinator and told her all about his behaviour towards me. She spoke to him and only then did his attitude towards me improve. But there were times when I would be working, and others around me talking, and he would direct the order to stop talking at me.

Q Why do you think this teacher singled you out from the remainder of the class?

A It could be anything. Even when my parents spoke to him at the parent/teacher interviews, he spoke down to them, in a demeaning manner. They were upset at his attitude, and he saw that, and dared to say to them, 'I suppose you are going to go speak to the co-ordinator!' My mother assured him that they would be going again to the co-ordinator, as his conduct was unacceptable.

Q What was the response of the co-ordinator?

A She simply assured us that she would resolve the matter.

"... there were times when I would be working, and others around me talking, and he would direct the order to stop talking at me."

"I would go home and feel like I was worthless... I kept having angry outbursts..."

Q Did the teacher's behaviour have an effect on you?

A Yes, definitely. I would go home and feel like I was worthless. I fought with my siblings and kept having angry outbursts without knowing what had caused them. My parents discussed with me again the possible reasons for me acting so out of character. We came to the conclusion that I felt insecure about myself because I knew I was doing the best I could do. I studied, did all my homework, yet it was never good enough. Sometimes you just know when you have done your best and when you can do better.

Q How did this affect things at home?

A My home life did suffer very much. My parents had to focus more on me than the other children. In this way they helped me over the difficult times, but the other children weren't given the attention they needed and would normally have received.

Q Are all the students in your class Catholic?

A Everyone except me. I am also the only one of my nationality in the class.

Q Do you believe that prejudice is involved here?

A Prejudice could be associated with the teacher's behaviour towards me.
At times I think it might be unless it is something else I can't identify.

Q Have you seen any signs of bullying by any other teacher?

A No, I can tell that all my other teachers like me. They are satisfied with my class performance, and they encourage me and give me confidence.

Q What do you believe you have learned from these experiences?

A I have learned that things aren't always what they seem. Even nasty people have reasons for being the way they are. Although that's no excuse to treat others badly, I think I will be more tolerant when I come across this type of behaviour again. I'm not saying I'll stand and take it, but I will try and understand that many times there are explanations for the way people act. There are reasons behind the cruel actions of others. I would not have learned that, if this girl hadn't treated me the way she did. My parents have helped me see things differently, and I have realised how lucky I am to have their interest and support. If the other girl had been as lucky as me, then all this wouldn't have happened.

Q How do you feel about the teacher's behaviour now?

A I think that whether the school is private or public, teachers have a duty of care - as my mother calls it. As adults, they are responsible for all of us. They are teaching us how to behave in the world, and how to behave with one another. I don't think it is right for them to single any child out and treat them differently. They should be building self-esteem in young people, not breaking it down. Again, I am very lucky that I have a supportive family, and that anger is something we can discuss and work through. For that I am really grateful. ■

"I am very lucky that I have a supportive family..."

Talking Points

◆ Having heard her bully's story Madeline understands a bit better why she was bullied. Do you think it's helpful to know this? Do you think bullying is ever excusable?

◆ Do you agree that the teacher's behaviour towards Madeline is a kind of bullying? How well do you think this matter was treated? What do you think a 'duty of care' entails? Are teachers there to look after the welfare of their pupils?

◆ What do you think about Madeline's attitude and behaviour? Pick out some of the things she says that help you to understand her personality.

It Happened to Miranda*

Photographs in this section are posed by models.

Miranda*, 17, became very self-conscious about her appearance as a result of what felt like verbal bullying by schoolmates at her independent girls-only school. Although it didn't happen a great deal it was enough for her to lose her confidence and added to her becoming anorexic, and later hospitalised. Her parents are separated.
* not her real name.

Q Did you always have a difficult time at school?

A Not at all. I enjoyed primary school. I had a lot of friends who seemed to like me in an uncritical way. So I didn't have any worries about going on to my next school. I knew it was an independent girls' school but I didn't think that would make it very different.

Q So did you have problems immediately?

A No for the first few weeks it was all right. Everyone was new and settling in but I was aware that the girls here were much more self-conscious and concerned with appearance and image than they had been in my first school.

Q Was that a problem for you? Were there things about you, physically, that you felt would be sneered at or criticised?

A I worried about my weight and thought people would see me as very chubby. I can see now that I really wasn't very large at all - maybe a dress size 12 while the girls I admired were probably size 10 - but people did make comments and I found myself thinking about my size quite a lot.

Q Were other girls really saying a lot about how you looked, or do you think it grew in your mind because you were anxious about it?

A I don't know that such a lot was said but when somebody did say something it really hit home. Also while I was in year six there was a very fat girl in the class and everyone seemed to hate her. I was frightened perhaps they would start talking about me in the same way.

"... people did make comments and I found myself thinking about my size quite a lot."

It's a Fact that...

Some victims of bullying are so distressed they commit or attempt to commit suicide.

Q So how did you deal with this?

A Well, it wasn't very nice but I started agreeing with the people saying things about the fat girl, like, She's so ugly,' 'She's gross' because I thought they would like me more and I thought I'd be one of them then.

Q Did it work?

A Well, not really because people could be nice one minute and not the next. The girls who felt powerful really used it. There was one who was a friend for a while but then she became spiteful. It upset me a lot and I used to cry uncontrollably a lot.

Q Did you not have any friends?

A I had some friends and they weren't at all unkind. Looking back now I don't know why that wasn't good enough, but it was the ones whose criticism I feared who had the most effect on me. I lost most of the confidence I had at primary school. I began to think more and more that if I could be thin then I would be admired and respected and I would feel much better.

Q Did you act on that thought?

A When I was 13 I started dieting and it got more and more extreme. I stopped eating at school during the day. I tried to keep it secret but people noticed. At home I ate very little and made it last a long time. My parents realised I wasn't eating much. They were worried and kept on at me about it so I developed some obsessional rituals around food. For instance, I'd find new yogurts and pour away half the contents

"... I'd find new yogurts and pour away half the contents then put the lid back on so my parents would think I was eating the whole thing."

then put the lid back on so my parents would think I was eating the whole thing. I'd slice fruit up very thinly and spread it over the plate and I'd eat some vegetables but that was about it.

Q Were you losing weight? How did your parents deal with this?

A My weight went down quite a lot and I must have become quite thin but I couldn't see that and just thought I must get thinner because then life would be all right. I know my parents realised I was distressed and they went to school to talk to the teachers to see what was wrong. But my teachers didn't know about the verbal bullying I'd had, and anyway teachers can't make people be friends with you.

Q So you were left to go on with your extreme dieting?

A No. My parents got more and more worried about me and they took me to a doctor, although I wasn't actually clinically underweight. I was referred to a psychiatrist which seemed stupid to me. I thought what I was doing was perfectly logical and sane. I was quite convinced that being thinner would get me the respect I so wanted from my schoolmates.
It seemed obvious to me that if you are thinner your body and face change and you become more interesting.

Q Did you start eating after seeing the psychiatrist?

A No. My parents tried to tempt me a lot with food. They came to school every day and brought me lunch. Then they sat in the car in the school car park and

watched me eat. Still I kept losing weight. I was driven and nothing else seemed as important.

It's a Fact that...

Incidences of bullying last an average of 37 seconds. The effects can last a lifetime.

Q How did the girls at school react as you lost weight?

A They were obviously aware of me getting thinner because I lost 19 kilograms. My friends didn't say anything and the ones who had made horrid remarks didn't either.

Q Were your parents even more desperate than before?

A They were. My mother took me to the doctor again and he had me in hospital the next day. I couldn't understand why. I thought I was all right. Then they photographed me in the hospital's eating disorders clinic and I saw that I looked like something out of a concentration camp. I was scared then.

Q Did you protest about being put in hospital?

A I was so exhausted I couldn't do anything. I could hardly get out of bed. Eventually I was moved from the children's ward to the adolescent unit, which was much better - and tougher. They wouldn't let me out of bed, or have any privileges, until they saw me eating. That made life very boring indeed so I decided I would eat again.

Q Did you start putting on weight?

A I did and I began to feel better and to see that really there weren't many choices: either I'd starve myself to death or I had to put on a bit of weight and deal with life that way.

Q How long were you out of school?

A A few weeks but when I reached six-and-a-half stone [41 kilograms] they seemed to think it was all right. I went back to school but I was still very weak at that weight. I couldn't concentrate and games exhausted me.

Q Did the doctors keep monitoring you?

A They did and because I still had a lot of obsessional behaviour they put me on the drug Seroxat. That numbed me. I started putting on weight until I became really quite chubby - bigger than I'd ever been.

"My friends didn't say anything and the ones who made horrid remarks didn't either."

It's a Fact that...

Males are more likely to be physically bullied while females are more likely to be verbally or psychologically bullied.

Q **So how did the girls at school treat you then?**

A In fact nobody said anything although when I really went on, a friend admitted I'd got a bit chubby. I had had some help which I think made me grow up and realise starving myself to death wasn't the way to deal with my problem.

Q **What help did you get?**

A My parents found an educational psychologist, Emily Lovegrove, who runs workshops on appearance-related bullying. She suggests strategies to help children at school. She also helps teachers and parents to find ways to deal with all kinds of bullying. She says that the kind of fairly subtle bullying I went through is quite common. I knew she was on my wavelength because she said things like it's difficult to go to a teacher in the way you might if someone was hitting you or stealing your money or shouting vile names. If you say that a girl is sneering at me, or someone called me chubby, you just feel it looks foolish.

Even from an early age, girls in particular can be subjected to appearance bullying.

"... the kind of quite subtle bullying I went through is quite common."

> "And if you feel good about who you are it gives an impotant message to others ..."

Q So what did the psychologist do with you?

A She talked to me about myself and she acknowledged that appearance does matter. That was important because when people say things like, 'Don't be silly - appearances don't matter,' it doesn't work because inside you know they do. But she also told me I looked good to her. And she got me to talk about the things I do like in myself. I found myself telling her I'm good at school work and generally she helped me build up a picture of all the positive things about myself.

She also showed me that you can change people's opinion of you by the way you react to them. Because bullying is so much about power if you don't let people feel they've got power over you by being nasty, then there's not much satisfaction in bullying you. And if you feel good about who you are it gives an important message to others and they will not see you as a victim.

Q So there was a lot of thinking about the psychology of how a bully may be feeling as well as behaving?

A Yes. The idea is to feel you can take charge of a situation and not let the person bullying do that. After a few sessions I found my confidence growing and with it my behaviour changed. I started walking more upright, I didn't hunch up as I had been doing before. I was told it's important to stand up and stand out. And the interesting thing is not only do other girls not say upsetting things but there seem to be far more people who want to be friends with me.

Q And what about your weight and how your look?

A I really have learnt to see my value in the other things I do and who I am. I can see that other things besides my weight matter in life. I no longer expect people to reject me. ■

Talking Points

- People at her school made a few comments about Miranda's weight, but she seems to have taken it very hard. Do you think this was 'subtle bullying' or was it more a problem she had about herself? Is bullying always as one-sided as it seems?

- Miranda thinks looks matter. Do you? Why?

- Miranda begins to bully another girl for being fat. What does this tell you about the nature of bullying?

It Happened to Jack

Jack, 14, was bullied by the brother of some friends at secondary school when he was 12. He says it wrecked the friendship with the boys and made him unhappy, but he helped himself by taking control of the situation. His mother, who also tells the story, recalls Jack being more distressed than he now remembers and the bullying was one of the reasons they changed his school. Jack lives in London, UK with his mother, father and sister.

Q Were you pleased to be moving to the comprehensive your parents had chosen?

A I was quite happy about it although I would have preferred more of my friends to be going, but only a couple came.

Q Did you find it easy to make new friends?

A I was a bit anxious about it but I soon got friendly with other kids and particularly twin boys my age. I was very keen on skateboarding and so were they. I remembered I had met them at a skateboarding party and we'd got on then.

Q Did these boys become important to you quite quickly?

A The second day at school they invited me to their house.

Q Did you enjoy that?

A It was fine at first although it wasn't a nice house. Very neglected, kind of wrecked looking and filthy, with things everywhere.

It's a Fact that...

Half of the victims of bullying tell no one: of those who do tell 47 per cent tell parents and 31 per cent a teacher. The other 22 per cent tell someone else they are close to.

Q Why do you think it was like that?

A I think it was because the parents had split up and things were unhappy, although the parents lived close to each other and the children could come and go. But the mother was never at home when I visited and there wasn't any tea for the brothers. They had chocolate bars and crisps and instant noodles, which they sorted out for themselves.

Q You say things were fine at first, but did that change?

A The brother of the boys, about four years older, came home and that was when things went wrong. I don't know why but he looked at me as though he hated me and said, 'Get out of my house.' I couldn't think of anything to say.

Q Did the brothers stick up for you?

A They tried a bit but I think they were intimidated by their brother. So I had to leave and walk home.

Q Were you upset?

A I was angry and upset when I got home because it was quite a long walk and it was cold and dark.

Q How did your parents react?

A I can't really remember but they were nice and tried to tell me not to worry.

Q Did you still spend much time with the brothers?

A We were really close in school and I had lots in common with them. We really liked each other. So when they asked me home again a few days later I thought I'd go. I didn't expect the same thing to happen again. I thought perhaps the brother had just been in a bad mood the last time.

Q So was the brother all right this time?

A No, he wasn't. As soon as he got home he just turned on me again and ordered me out. I didn't think he would hurt me physically but it was nasty and I felt scared. The boys seemed too scared to protest so I went.

Q So did you go to the boys' house any more?

A I started going but leaving before the brother came back. Even then I felt very uncomfortable and scared but I wanted to be with my friends.

"... I felt very scared but I wanted to be with my friends."

"Things suddenly got worse and he hunted me down and said nasty things if he saw me."

Q Was the boy physically menacing?

A He was big, really big and he didn't seem to have any friends so he was very possessive about his brothers. He made it clear he wasn't going to let me get close to them. But I know he didn't intimidate all the twins' friends, and I don't know why he picked on me because he never said anything. He didn't try to get to know me at all.

Q Was he at the same school?

A Yes, he was and he bullied me there as well. If he saw me with the brothers he would tell me to leave them alone. It seemed to matter to him a lot to have control. But at school it wasn't so bad because he didn't have power there.

Q Anywhere else?

A He used to appear at the skateboarding area where all of us who were keen on that sport gathered. He would just pick on me every time.

It's a Fact that...

Researchers suggest that twice as many children are bullied in the school environment than in any other location.

Q Did you tell your parents about it?

A I did and my mum rang my form tutor about it and the tutor rang the boy who was intimidating. I knew that because things suddenly got worse and he hunted me down and said nasty things if he saw me. I was cross my mum had done that.

Q Did you go to the twins' house any more?

A They suggested it a few times but I said no because of their brother but they didn't seem to understand. It wasn't nice thinking he'd come along any time and be horrible. Thinking back, he may have disliked me because he was a bit left out when I was there. I suppose he had his brothers to be with when they were alone.

Q So that was the end of the visits?

A I decided to try once more. But it was just the same story. The brother opened the door and told me to get out. It was winter, about 7 p.m. and it was very cold and dark and it was raining. I wanted to ring my mum and ask her to pick me up because it was about a 20 minute walk on the skateboard to get home, but I wasn't allowed to phone.

Q Were your parents upset?

A They were pretty annoyed. They had said, after the other times I was sent out, that I should stop going to the house, but I wanted to be with these boys. They were important to me and they lived near the skateboarding area and that was where they went after school. But after that I realised it wasn't worth having them as best friends if the brother was going to make it so hard.

Q So what did you do?

A I started being friendlier with other children and the friendship with the twins ended. The brother left me alone and I certainly felt happier knowing he wasn't a threat any longer.

Q Did you have any bad feelings left by what happened?

A I felt it was wrong that he had been able to spoil being a skateboarder for me and that he had broken up a good friendship. I know it's not as bad as physical bullying but it made me miserable.

Q Your parents decided you should move schools at the end of that year. Was that because of the bullying?

A I think it was a bit, but more because it wasn't a

Photograph posed by models.

"They were important to me and they lived near the skateboarding area and that was where they went after school."

good school. Whatever the reasons I'm much happier at my new school and the friendships I've got are easy. There's no bullying.

JACK'S MOTHER

Q Were you happy about the friends Jack made when he moved to secondary school?

A I didn't know much about them, only that they were extreme skateboarders and there was a whole group. They would go off on skate trips and it was very important to Jack to be in the group. I knew it was important to let him. They all went off to this place where you could skateboard and it was near where the others all lived, but we were in a different direction, about half an hour's walk away.

"... it was very important to Jack to be in the group."

It's a Fact that...

Boys are more likely to be bullies than girls.

Bullies tend to have average social popularity up to about the age of 14 or 15. However by late adolescence their popularity begins to fall.

Q Did you see Jack's very close bond with the twins as a good thing?

A I had nothing against the boys but their home life appeared chaotic. Since their parents separated, the older brother, who I never met, refused to see the father. The mother had MS and I had the impression she was falling apart. It was pretty dysfunctional I think.

Q So life was very different for them than for Jack?

A The twins were given a great deal more freedom than we would give our children. Arrangements with them seemed to be pretty loose and there didn't seem to be much structure to their lives.

Q Did you try to steer Jack away from these friends?

A We didn't because he was desperate to be in this group and, although he was young, that year when they move into secondary school children tend to feel they need to show they are grown up. And at first we didn't see it as a problem.

Q When did you?

A There was a string of incidents involving the elder brother. He would either order Jack away from the communal area, where they skateboarded, and because he was being victimised people joined in grabbing his skateboard. Or Jack was ordered out when they went to the house. It was getting to be winter and cold, and Jack didn't feel he could stand up to the brother. He would come home incredibly upset, but not able to articulate what it was about.

Q Was there anything else?

A Well, the boys would invite Jack for sleepovers, for example, and he'd get very excited with great expectations, then at the last minute it didn't happen. I suspect there had never been any arrangements made with the parents. He would get very low then.

Q What did you do to help Jack with all these upsets?

A I comforted him and tried to make him realise it wasn't his fault but it was certainly making him unhappy.

Q Did you think of stopping him going to the skateboarding area and the twins' house?

A We certainly talked to him about that and suggested he would feel much better if he didn't expose himself to the brother, but he didn't want to be frightened off and it seemed important for him to work things out for himself.

Q Did things come to a head?

A Yes, the time Jack was ordered out of the twins' house on a freezing, wet night. The bullying went on over about five months and

"... it seemed important for [Jack] to work things out for himself."

> "... [Jack] was getting to be more anxious. He wasn't as upbeat and optimistic as he had been."

it was coming up to winter and through winter. On this occasion he was very cold and wet and I think he felt more upset and powerless than any other time.

Q **Did that have a lasting effect?**

A I had been aware of his confidence being affected by the brother and he was starting to withdraw into himself. I could see he was getting to be more anxious. He wasn't as upbeat and optimistic as he had been.

Q **Did that affect you?**

A Yes, I became anxious too, worrying what would happen to him each day. And his reaction to that was to tell me less and less.

Q **Did you feel there was anything you could do about the boy?**

A I decided that, as some of the nastiness was happening in the playground and the rest was happening through people at the school, they should know. So I went to see the form tutor and Jack came too. The school were nice enough and said they would contact the boy's mother, although I'm not sure they ever did. And to be honest I don't think it would have helped: I think that's where the problem was.

Q **Did you feel you needed to act?**

A Jack's father and I talked quite a lot about what to do and we started looking at other schools. Then in spring, almost like a conscious decision, Jack moved away from the twins and that group.

Q So were you happy to leave him at the school?

A No. We weren't terribly pleased with the teaching anyway, and I felt the bullying had spoiled the place for him. So we discussed it with Jack and he clearly wasn't unhappy to leave.

Q Was that a good decision?

A Absolutely. Within days he was much more at ease, confident, cheery as he had been in the past. And it's gone on that way. There really doesn't seem to be unpleasantness at the school and he has some good friends.

Q Do you feel the incident is completely finished with now?

A I think Jack has grown up so much in the past two years he probably doesn't recognise his younger self of then. And when humiliating things like that happen you don't really want to remember them.

Q And from your point of view?

A I feel very happy about Jack, but the bullying time has taught me how powerless you are as a parent in this situation. You can't tell the child who is bullying to be nice, and it almost certainly won't work to ask the parents to make the child be nice. I've come to the conclusion the only thing you can really do is to make home a very safe and nurturing place and give your child the courage to go back out into the world by themself. ■

"... the bullying time has taught me how powerless you are as a parent..."

Talking Points

◆ Do Jack and his mum see what happened in the same way?

◆ Jack's mum feels there's little that parents can do to help their bullied children. Do you agree? Is parental intervention a bad idea?

◆ Jack was mainly bullied at his friends' house. Do you think it's a school's responsibility to deal with bullying that goes on outside its gates?

◆ Was Jack right to make new friends? How would you have dealt with the same situation?

It Happened to Sarah

Sarah, 18, was bullied at secondary school. She then bullied other children before moving schools. Once she had moved and was happier she trained as a peer mediator and helped other children sort out their bullying problems. She grew up living with her mother and then her grandmother. She lives in Leicester and is studying computers at college.

Q How was your time at primary school?

A That was fine and for secondary I went to the local school with a lot of friends. But a year later I moved and had to go to a different secondary school.

Q Was that different to your other school?

A The students weren't as friendly and I didn't feel I fitted in as well. It was difficult because I was new and everyone else was into their second year.

Q Did you feel you were singled out?

A At first it was all right because there was a group of girls I started to hang around with and we got on all right. Then something went wrong but I still don't know why.

Q So what happened when things went wrong?

A They began calling me names, pushing me around physically and making it very plain that they were against me and I wasn't part of their group.

Q How did that affect you?

A It made me very miserable. I didn't want to be in school because it was in lessons that quite a lot of the bullying went on. It was name-calling, they threw things at me. I felt very isolated and unhappy. I started to skip school.

Q Did the teachers realise you were being bullied?

A They didn't seem to realise and they didn't bother to find out. They just put me on report loads of times for not being in school. And I was scared of telling them because I thought that if the girls bullying me got into trouble, they would come back on me. There was a tough culture in the school. I saw others being beaten up.

"I was scared of telling them because I thought that if the girls bullying me got into trouble they would come back on me."

Q Did you tell your mum what was going on?

A I didn't. My mum believes that you have to stand up for yourself. If someone hits you - hit back. If you can't do that, tell a teacher. I thought if I told her she would go to the teacher even if I didn't want her to. She wouldn't have understood how it would come back on me.

It's a Fact that...

By age 24, up to 60 per cent of people who are identified as childhood bullies have at least one criminal conviction.

In the USA it is estimated that 160,000 children skip school each day because of intimidation by their peers.

Children who have been bullied are more likely to bully other people.

Q So your mum never knew what was going on?

A Not until a few years later when I was on a television programme talking about what had happened. It was the first she knew of it and she told me how upset she was to think of me going through that. She said she wished I'd told her and that she could have helped.

Q Did things remain the same at school or did they change?

A I was bullied for about nine months and it really knocked my confidence. Then one day I got into a bit of an argument with a

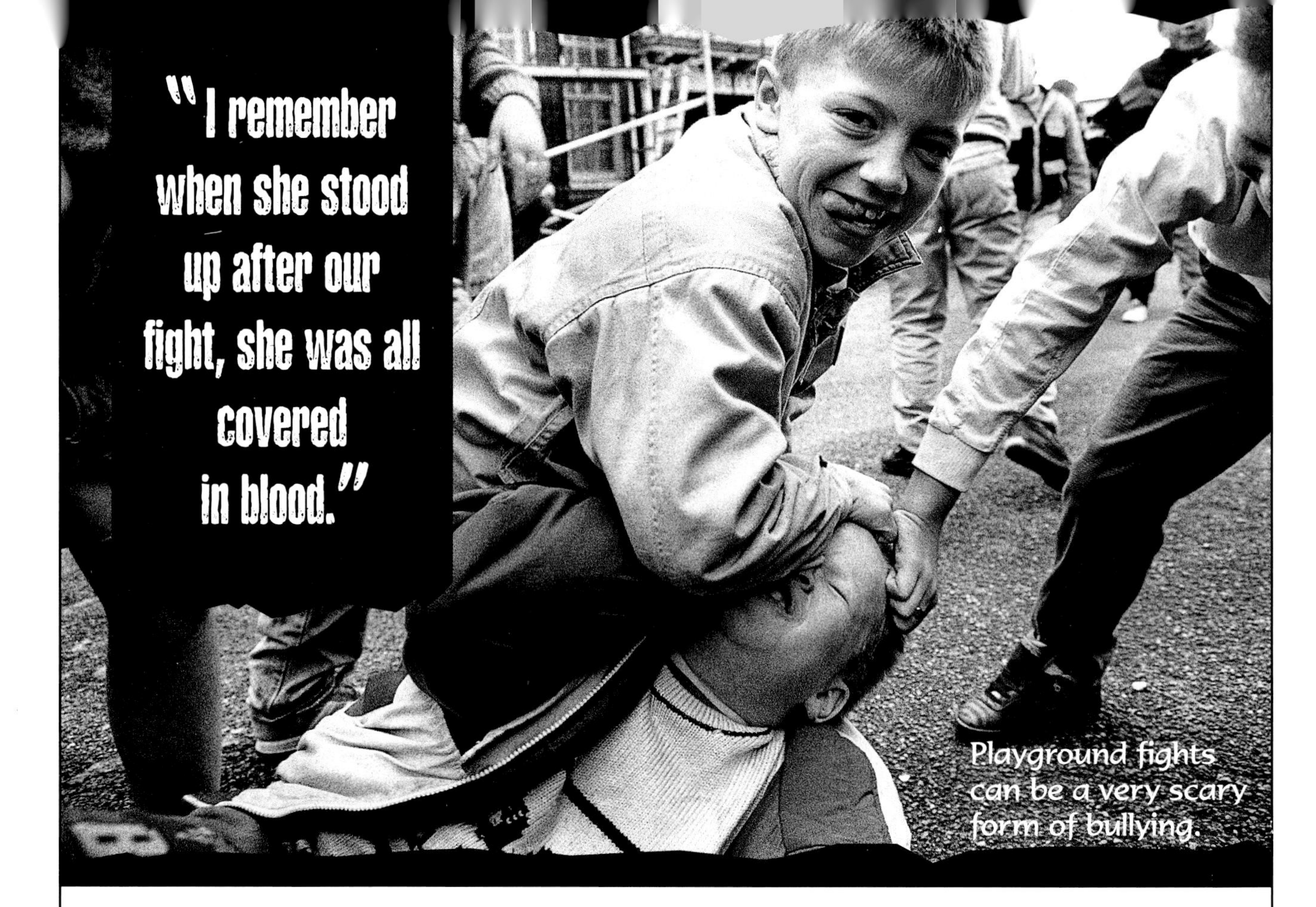

Playground fights can be a very scary form of bullying.

girl who had left the school but was outside for some reason. Then, suddenly, all the girls who had been bullying me crowded around and egged me on to beat her up. So I did. We had a physical fight, and she ended up in hospital. I remember when she stood up after our fight, she was all covered in blood. I'd split her face and she had to have stitches.

Q Had you done anything like this before?

A No. Never but I think it was the combination of having all the angry upset feelings bottled up inside me and having the girls who had been so horrid to me on my side, wanting me to fight. It was very confusing.

Q Did you feel bad about what you had done?

A Not at the time. I didn't think about her because the thing that mattered was I gained more respect from the girls who had been bullying me. Other people outside school said the girl I had beaten up was very angry and would press charges with the police.

Q Wasn't that frightening?

A I wasn't frightened. I think I was on quite a high. There was a bit of a buzz to having found power. I realised I enjoyed bullying, although I usually picked on people younger and weaker than me. Sometimes I just had arguments and did a bit of pushing but often I got into fights with someone I knew I could beat. I was about 13 at the time.

Q Did you get into trouble with the school?

A I did a bit but that wasn't as important as the fact that I gained more respect from the girls who had bullied me, each time I bullied other girls or won a fight. And it felt exciting after being bullied to know I had power and was admired by others for it.

Q Did you think at all about how it felt to the people you were bullying?

A Not then while I was doing it. I was completely focused on my own feelings. In my head was the thought that I had been through it all, so why shouldn't someone else? I think I was actually very confused at the time.

"I gained more respect from the girls who had bullied me, each time I bullied other girls..."

It's a Fact that...

Students who are sometimes hit at home and those who spend their time without adults are more likely to bully their peers.

Q So did your bullying go on and get worse?

A I think it would have done but in fact things were difficult at home, so I decided to move in with my grandmother. Her home was near my old school, so it was decided I should go there again. I was happy about that because I had a lot of friends there who I didn't see often. And actually once I'd gone I felt quite relieved.

Q So were you bullied or did you bully back at your old school?

A No. I immediately got in with my old friends and felt much happier.

Q So you had nothing to do with bullying after that?

A I did in a different way. One day two co-ordinators from an organisation called CRISP came into the school. They talked about the work they do training school pupils to work as peer mediators - to develop skills to help other children who are caught up in bullying. This can work better than a teacher deciding what should be done.

Q What effect did that have on you?

A I was very interested and felt that peer mediation was something I could do because I had been on both sides, as a victim and a bully, and so I would understand how both sides felt in a dispute.

Q So what happened then?

A The co-ordinators asked anyone interested in being a peer mediator to go for an interview. I went and told them all about what had happened with me. Out of all the people who applied only a few got chosen and I was one of them.

Q So you were offered the chance to train?

A Yes. We had a weekend of residential training. They talked a lot about the feelings of bullies as well as those who are bullied, and what may lie behind bullying. It was very interesting. We were taught to listen and communicate effectively and how to deal with challenging behaviour. We learnt about using eye contact and body language to create the right atmosphere.

Q So what happened then?

A They set up mediation sessions in the school. Sometimes it was difficult to get people who were at loggerheads to come but usually people were willing to try. We would get the bully and the victim to sit down with us - I worked with another student so there were always two of us. This means that the people with problems feel that there isn't a power imbalance - there's two mediators and two parties.

Q How did it work?

A We would talk to them and try to find out the source of the problem and how they might sort it out. The important thing is for both parties to be given a chance to express what is going on with them.

Q So did you then suggest solutions?

A No. Peer mediators are not there to tell people what to do, but to help them come to a way of sorting out the situation themselves. CRISP explained that it's not about trying to get people to be friends, unless they want to. The agreement might be that they are not going to push each other or speak to each other in the corridor - in other words to avoid the behaviour that leads to the bullying.

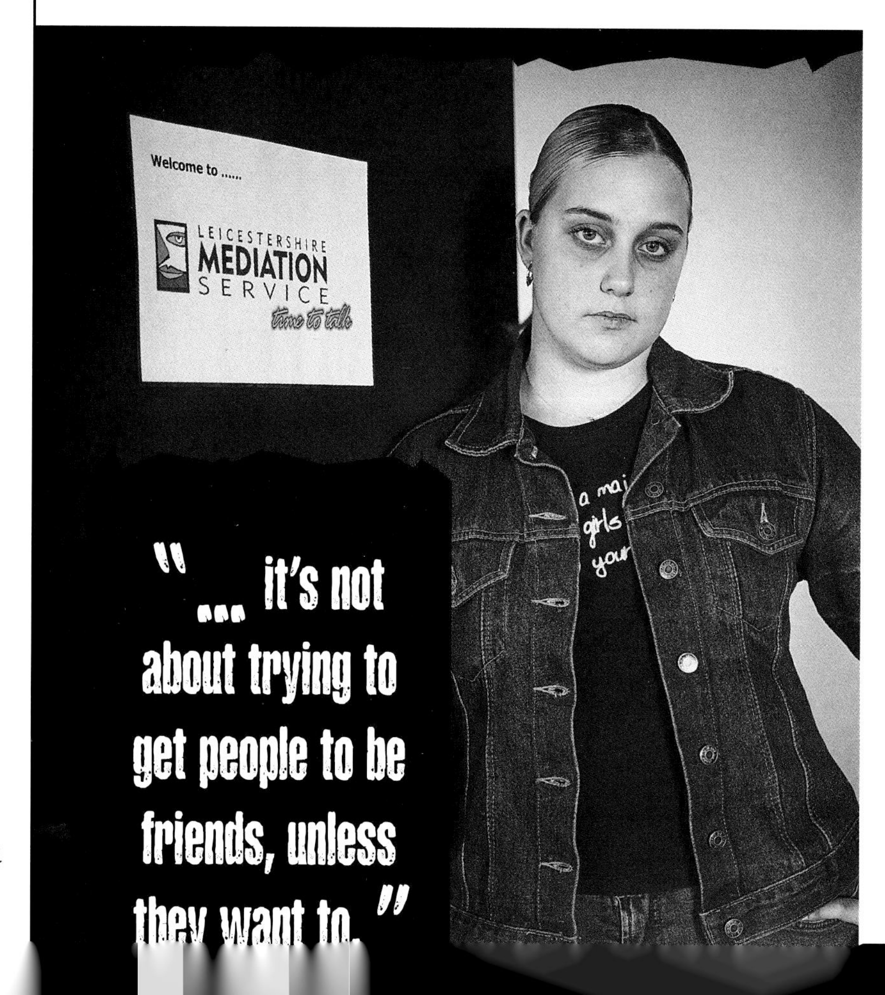

"... it's not about trying to get people to be friends, unless they want to."

"My experience of that school could have been so much happier..."

It's a Fact that...

Schools that introduce anti-bullying programmes with parent, teacher and community support have found a 50 per cent reduction in direct bullying a year after implementation.

Q What happens if the people argue?

A We would explain that the process couldn't work if they behaved like that and that we had to agree ground rules. We would draw up a form saying no intimidating, no bad language, no fighting and so on. The students had to sign it at the mediation. When they came reluctantly we explained how it would benefit them if they could find a way to sort out their problems. In the end most chose to do it.

Q How long did you do this for?

A I did it for three years until I left school. CRISP did an evaluation by talking to students a couple of months after mediation about how things were. They found quite a high success rate, with students keeping to their agreements.

Q So did it all finish when you left school?

A No. Now I'm at college I do a bit of training and delivering programmes to schools through CRISP.

Q Do you think peer mediation would have helped you when you were being bullied?

A I'm sure it would have made a big difference. My experience of that school could have been so much happier if the bullying had been sorted out. ■

Talking Points

◆ Sarah's mother believes that you should stand up to bullies, by fighting back if necessary. Do you agree with this? Why?

◆ Anti-bullying mediation like the one at Sarah's school is usually very effective. Why do you think these programmes work so well? Should every school have one?

◆ When Sarah was bullying she only thought about her feelings and not those of the people she bullied. Do you think this is how bullies usually feel?

Useful addresses and contacts

UK

NSPCC

The National Society for the Prevention of Cruelty to Children is the UK's leading charity specialising in child protection and prevention of cruelty to children. Bullying is one of the issues that the NSPCC takes very seriously.

NSPCC
42 Curtain Road
London EC2A 3NH
Hotline: 0808 800 5000
www.nspcc.org.uk

Kidscape

One of the main aims of this organisation is to prevent bullying. They offer support and solutions to bullying issues through publications, conferences and a helpline.

Kidscape
2 Grosvenor Gardens
London SW1W OOH
Helpline: 08451 205204
www.kidscape.org.uk

Bullying Online

This is a clearly set out website offering advice for parents, teachers and children involved in bullying issues. It also lays out legal advice and includes many tips on how to overcome the problem.

www.bullying.co.uk

De-fuse

Anti-bullying workshops run by psychologist Emily Lovegrove.

Contact: defuse@btopenworld.com

CRISP (Conflict Resolution in Schools Programme)

Provides training and resources to manage conflict and bullying.

www.crispuk.org

Department for Education and Skills

This government department offers publications for teachers and parents concerned about bullying issues.

Department for Education and Skills
Sanctuary Buildings
Great Smith Street
London SW1P 3BT
www.dfes.gov/uk

Childline

Childline is a registered charity that runs a free and confidential telephone and website hotline for children to ring, in case of need.

Helpline: 0800 1111
www.childine.org.uk

AUSTRALIA

Kidshelp

A charity that runs a telephone helpline for children in need.

Helpline: 1800 55 1800
www.kidshelp.com.au

Bullying Noway

This website was created by the Australian educational community to work together for every child to feel safe.

www.bullyingnoway.com.au

Glossary

anorexia nervosa
A medical condition where the person becomes obsessed by their weight and appearance, and hardly eats. Without treatment, it can lead to starvation and death.

assault
A violent physical or verbal attack.

assessment
A report drawn up by a doctor or psychologist giving the medical view on the person's condition and recommending what action needs to be taken.

Attention-Deficit Disorder
A condition that can affect children. It describes children who have an abnormal lack of ability to concentrate for more than a short period of time.

attention-seeker
A person who, through the way they behave, seeks to attract a lot of attention to himself or herself.

behavioural problem
The name for a range of problems that some people suffer from where they find it difficult to behave in an acceptable way.

bullying
Persecution of another through name-calling (verbal bullying), making comments about the way someone looks (appearance-related bullying), or by actually attacking and hurting someone (physical bullying).

discrimination
To treat someone differently because of their appearance, sex, race or religion.

dyslexia
A disorder that causes learning difficulty in reading, spelling or numeracy. It is sometimes called 'word blindness'.

intimidation
The use of violence or threats to influence the behaviour of someone else, or force them to do something.

manipulator
A person who seeks to control people or events to their own advantage, sometimes through deception.

mediator
A person who intervenes between two people or groups to try to find ways of making them talk to each other and solve their differences.

peer group
A group of people of the same age or ability.

penalise
To impose a punishment on somebody.

prejudice
To form an unreasonable opinion of someone quickly, without really knowing them, or to have an unreasonable preference of one group over another.

racism
Belief in the superiority of some racial groups over others.

self-esteem
A good opinion of oneself - self-respect.

victim
In this case, the person who has done nothing but is being bullied.

victimisation
To single out someone for ill-treatment.

Index

Getting active!

On your own:
Write a paragraph to explain whether you agree or disagree with the following statement: 'A bit of mild bullying is no bad thing - it toughens children up and prepares them for life as an adult.'

In pairs:
Do a survey in your school of pupils' experiences of bullying. Think of at least five questions to ask, such as: Have you ever been bullied? How often? Have you ever participated in bullying?

In groups:
If your school does not already have one, put together a plan for starting a peer-mediation service. First, read the interview with Sarah on pages 40–45. Then write a proposal for your headteacher. Include all the advantages, but also think about the possible difficulties, such as finding the right people and environment, and who will organise and manage the service.